THE CONSTITUTIONAL CONVENTION

CREATING THE CONSTITUTION

BY JILL KEPPELER

Gareth Stevens
PUBLISHING

Please visit our website, www.garethstevens.com. For a free color catalog of all our high-quality books, call toll free 1-800-542-2595 or fax 1-877-542-2596.

Library of Congress Cataloging-in-Publication Data

Names: Keppeler, Jill, author.
Title: Creating the Constitution / Jill Keppeler.
Description: New York : Gareth Stevens Publishing, 2021. | Series: The
    Constitution explained! | Includes index.
Identifiers: LCCN 2020004008 | ISBN 9781538258484 (library binding) | ISBN
    9781538258460 (paperback) | ISBN 9781538258477 (6 Pack) | ISBN 9781538258491
    (ebook)
Subjects: LCSH: United States. Constitutional Convention (1787)–Juvenile
    literature. | Constitutional history–United States–18th
    century–Juvenile literature.
Classification: LCC KF4510 . K47 2020 | DDC 342.7302/92–dc23
LC record available at https://lccn.loc.gov/2020004008

First Edition

Published in 2021 by
Gareth Stevens Publishing
111 East 14th Street, Suite 349
New York, NY 10003

Copyright © 2021 Gareth Stevens Publishing

Designer: Sarah Liddell
Editor: Therese Shea

Photo credits: Cover, p. 1 Dan Thornberg/Shutterstock.com; background texture used throughout Lukasz Szwaj/Shutterstock.com; p. 5 Alex Wong/Staff/Getty Images News/ Getty Images; p. 7 Smith Collection/Gado/Contributor/Archive Photos/Getty Images; p. 9 Fine Art/Contributor/Corbis Historical/Getty Images; p. 11 UniversalImagesGroup/ Contributor/Universal Images Group/Getty Images; p. 13 Hulton Archive/Stringer/ Archive Photos/Getty Images; p. 15 Danita Delimont/Gallo Images/Getty Images Plus/Getty Images; p. 17 Win McNamee/Staff/Getty Images News/Getty Images; p. 19 PSboom/Shutterstock.com; p. 21 Pgiam/E+/Getty Images; p. 23 (*The Federalist*) Fotosearch/Stringer/Archive Photos/Getty Images; p. 23 (Alexander Hamilton) Buyenlarge/Contributor/Archive Photos/Getty Images; p. 25 MPI/Stringer/Archive Photos/Getty Images; p. 27 Stock Montage/Contributor/Archive Photos/Getty Images.

Printed in the United States of America

Some of the images in this book illustrate individuals who are models. The depictions do not imply actual situations or events.

CPSIA compliance information: Batch #CS20GS: For further information contact Gareth Stevens, New York, New York at 1-800-542-2595.

Find us on

CONTENTS

WORDS IN THE GLOSSARY APPEAR IN **BOLD** TYPE
THE FIRST TIME THEY ARE USED IN THE TEXT.

A PIECE OF
HISTORY

In Washington, DC, a huge chamber under a high, round ceiling is located on the upper level of the National Archives Museum. Three old **documents** are on display in this special room. These pieces of paper are original copies of the Declaration of Independence, the U.S. Constitution, and the Bill of Rights.

Looking at the four yellowed pieces of **parchment** that make up the Constitution, you might wonder why words written more than 200 years ago are so important. However, there's a lot behind those words, from the large "We the People" written at the top of the first page to the 39 names at the end. Let's go back to 1787 and learn about how the U.S. Constitution came to be.

THE ROTUNDA

The documents are kept in the Rotunda of the Charters of Freedom. The rotunda is a large, round room with a domed ceiling, or a ceiling that looks like half of a ball. The room is kept cold and somewhat dark, because these conditions help preserve the old parchment and the writing on it. No one can take photographs in the chamber because light from flash photography may fade the ink.

GUARDS STAND NEXT TO THE ORIGINAL COPIES OF THE U.S. CONSTITUTION, THE DECLARATION OF INDEPENDENCE, AND THE BILL OF RIGHTS IN THE NATIONAL ARCHIVES MUSEUM IN WASHINGTON, DC.

A CLOSER LOOK

TOGETHER, THE DECLARATION OF INDEPENDENCE, THE CONSTITUTION, AND THE BILL OF RIGHTS MAKE UP THE U.S. CHARTERS OF FREEDOM. A CHARTER IS A KIND OF LEGAL DOCUMENT.

BEFORE THE CONSTITUTION

Did you know the United States had a different constitution before the U.S. Constitution? The **Continental Congress** approved the Articles of Confederation in 1777, a year after the American colonies declared independence from Great Britain. That early constitution was ratified, or officially approved, by the states on March 1, 1781, before the American Revolution was over.

The Articles of Confederation bound the new states together in a loose confederation. A confederation is a league in which each member provides support for the others and yet maintains independence. The Articles gave Congress a number of powers (including the power to deal with other countries and make money), but it didn't have the power to make the states follow laws or pay taxes. The federal, or national, government wasn't effective.

Under the Articles of Confederation, the states were largely independent and often could ignore the U.S. government. Eventually, the federal government's lack of power under the Articles led to big problems for the United States. The country needed a stronger national government that could collect taxes, manage finances, and deal with certain problems, such as Shays' Rebellion, a series of protests that took place in Massachusetts in 1786 and 1787.

JOHN DICKINSON OF PENNSYLVANIA BEGAN TO WRITE THE FIRST DRAFT OF THE ARTICLES OF CONFEDERATION IN 1776.

To all to whom

A CLOSER LOOK

WITH THE MEMORIES OF BRITISH AUTHORITY STILL FRESH, MANY PEOPLE IN THE YOUNG UNITED STATES WERE CONCERNED ABOUT HAVING A STRONG NATIONAL GOVERNMENT. THIS IS ONE OF THE REASONS FOR THE WEAKNESSES OF THE ARTICLES OF CONFEDERATION.

GATHERING IN PHILADELPHIA

Delegates from the states were invited to a **convention** to amend the Articles of Confederation in Philadelphia, Pennsylvania. The meeting opened May 14, 1787, at the Pennsylvania State House. Only delegates from two states, Pennsylvania and Virginia, were there. It wasn't until May 25 that there were enough delegates to start.

Many delegates didn't even show up. Only 55 of the 74 delegates in total attended the convention. The New Hampshire group arrived two months late. Still, the delegates who were there on May 25 got to work. They nominated George Washington to lead the convention. They also named a group of men, including Alexander Hamilton, to come up with rules for the gathering. Some delegates were already talking about creating a new constitution rather than amending the old one.

A CLOSER LOOK

THE MOVE TOWARD AMENDING THE ARTICLES OF CONFEDERATION STARTED EARLIER, AT THE ANNAPOLIS CONVENTION. THIS MEETING OF STATE REPRESENTATIVES TOOK PLACE IN SEPTEMBER 1786 IN ANNAPOLIS, MARYLAND.

RHODE ISLAND, THE ROGUE ISLAND?

One state never sent any delegates to the Constitutional Convention—Rhode Island. The state's leaders didn't like the idea of a stronger central government. They thought the convention was a way to overthrow the existing government. Years later, in May 1790, the so-called "Rogue Island" would be the last state to ratify the U.S. Constitution. Rhode Island's first representative finally joined Congress more than a year after the first session began.

THE DELEGATES WHO MET AT THE PENNSYLVANIA STATE HOUSE, SHOWN HERE IN THE LATE 1800s, DID SO IN SECRECY. GUARDS KEPT PEOPLE AWAY.

THE VIRGINIA PLAN

On May 29, 1787, delegate Edmund Randolph, who was also the governor of Virginia, outlined a plan for a new constitution and government. James Madison, another Virginia delegate, had drafted the plan. This proposal featured three branches of government—executive, legislative, and judicial—each of which could check the power of the other two. It also called for a bicameral legislature, or a law-making body with two houses, with representation based on a state's population or wealth.

The Committee of the Whole, the name for the whole group of delegates, **debated** the Virginia Plan, as it was called. It contrasted with the New Jersey Plan, presented by New Jersey delegate William Paterson, which called for simply improving the Articles and for equal representation for states in Congress.

A CLOSER LOOK

THE DELEGATES DIDN'T CONSIDER THE NEW JERSEY PLAN LONG. HOWEVER, THE CALL FOR EQUAL REPRESENTATION FOR STATES IN CONGRESS WOULD REMAIN AN IMPORTANT IDEA THROUGHOUT THE CONVENTION.

THE FATHER OF THE CONSTITUTION

Founding Father James Madison took notes of the Constitutional Convention every day. He had studied history and politics to figure out a way to deal with the issues of the young United States, and he had decided the country needed a stronger central government. Later, people would call him the Father of the Constitution. He would go on to write the Bill of Rights and become the fourth president of the United States.

JAMES MADISON WAS BORN IN 1751 AND DIED IN 1836. HE WAS PRESIDENT FROM 1809 TO 1817. AT THE TIME OF THE CONSTITUTIONAL CONVENTION, HE WAS 36 YEARS OLD.

A QUESTION OF REPRESENTATION

As time went on, it became clear that the convention would be creating an entirely new constitution rather than amending the Articles of Confederation. Delegates continued the debate about fair representation in the proposed new Congress. Those from the large, populated states said that it must be according to population. Those from the small, less populated states insisted on equal representation for all the states, no matter how many people they had. How slaves should be counted in a state's population was a key part of this debate.

The debates sometimes became angry. Delegates made accusations against other delegates and even threatened them. Members worried that the convention would fall apart. Even the normally calm George Washington became upset. Neither side would yield on the issue.

A CLOSER LOOK

DELEGATE ALEXANDER HAMILTON OF NEW YORK ALSO PROPOSED A PLAN FOR GOVERNMENT. HOWEVER, IT WAS VERY LIKE THE BRITISH GOVERNMENT AND DIDN'T GET MUCH SUPPORT.

Luther Martin, a lawyer and delegate from Maryland, spoke out on the issue of equal representation in the new Congress. He didn't like the Virginia Plan. In fact, one day of the convention, he spoke for three hours against it. He said, "The states have a right to an equality of representation. This is secured to us by our present articles of confederation; we are in possession of this privilege."

GEORGE WASHINGTON, SHOWN IN THIS DRAWING OF THE CONSTITUTIONAL CONVENTION, WAS ANNOYED OVER THE CONSTANT ARGUING. HE CALLED THOSE WHO WERE AGAINST A STRONG CENTRAL GOVERNMENT "NARROW MINDED POLITICIANS."

THE GREAT COMPROMISE

Finally, a few delegates, including Oliver Ellsworth and Roger Sherman of Connecticut, proposed what became known as the Great Compromise, or sometimes the Connecticut Compromise. They suggested a bicameral legislature with the representation in one house (the House of Representatives) determined by state population and the representation in the other house (the Senate) equal for all states. It worked—barely. The states present approved the Great Compromise by one vote. This saved the future of the Constitutional Convention. It wasn't the only compromise to take place, however.

Delegates also compromised on a way to count slaves in the population of each state: three-fifths of the slaves would be counted toward representation in the House. Other issues of slavery would come back to haunt the convention.

A CLOSER LOOK

EDMUND RANDOLPH OF THE COMMITTEE OF DETAIL LATER BECAME THE FIRST U.S. **ATTORNEY GENERAL**. ELLSWORTH, RUTLEDGE, AND WILSON BECAME SUPREME COURT JUSTICES.

THE COMMITTEE OF DETAIL

The week after the delegates approved the Great Compromise they selected a Committee of Detail to draft a new constitution on July 24, 1787. The members were John Rutledge of South Carolina who led the committee, Nathaniel Gorham of Massachusetts, James Wilson of Pennsylvania, Edmund Randolph, and Oliver Ellsworth. While the committee worked on the draft, the rest of the delegates got a break. The whole convention met again on August 6.

THE FIRST SESSION OF CONGRESS UNDER THE U.S. CONSTITUTION BEGAN IN 1789. NORTH CAROLINA AND RHODE ISLAND HADN'T RATIFIED THE CONSTITUTION YET, SO THEY DIDN'T HAVE REPRESENTATIVES IN THE SENATE AND HOUSE AT FIRST.

CONGRESS, THEN AND NOW

SENATE IN 1789:
22 SENATORS

HOUSE OF REPRESENTATIVES IN 1789:
59 REPRESENTATIVES

SENATE TODAY:
100 SENATORS (FROM 50 STATES)

HOUSE OF REPRESENTATIVES TODAY:
435 REPRESENTATIVES

15

DRAFTS AND DETAILS

When the delegates met again on August 6, it was time for more debate. They argued about the draft of the Constitution piece by piece, every **clause** and sentence. They talked about the powers of the executive, or president, and the judicial branch, which would take the form of a Supreme Court and lower federal courts. They argued about who would oversee **commerce** among the states.

The issue of slavery returned as well. Delegates had different feelings about slavery. One proposed a tax on importing slaves. Others thought the issue should be ignored for a time because it could tear the convention apart. In the end, delegates from the Southern states and the New England states made a deal to allow importation of slaves for at least another 20 years.

A CLOSER LOOK

ABOLITIONIST SAMUEL HOPKINS WAS UPSET "THAT THESE STATES, WHO HAVE BEEN FIGHTING FOR LIBERTY AND CONSIDER THEMSELVES AS THE HIGHEST AND MOST NOBLE EXAMPLE OF **ZEAL** FOR IT, CANNOT AGREE IN ANY CONSTITUTION, UNLESS IT INDULGE AND AUTHORIZE THEM TO ENSLAVE THEIR FELLOW MEN."

While the deal on slavery worked to save the Constitution, it didn't make anyone happy. Ten states in the country had already outlawed slavery, although Georgia and the Carolinas had not and threatened to leave the convention. These states also worked to be sure the Constitution had a clause promising fugitive slaves would be returned to the South. Abolitionists were furious, and some refused to support the Constitution, believing it was a proslavery document.

MANY DELEGATES WROTE NOTES ON THEIR COPIES OF THE CONSTITUTION. A COPY BELONGING TO GEORGE WASHINGTON IS SHOWN HERE.

[15]

or cause, the court shall neverthelefs proceed to pronounce judgment. The judgment shall be final and conclusive. The proceedings shall be transmitted to the President of the Senate, and shall be lodged among the public records for the security of the parties concerned. Every commissioner shall, before he sit in judgment, take an oath, to be administered by one of the judges of the supreme or superior court of the State where the cause shall be tried, " well " and truly to hear and determine the matter in question, according to the " beft of his judgment, without favour, affection, or hope of reward."

Strike out

Strike out.

Sect. 3. All controversies concerning lands claimed under different grants of two or more States, whose jurisdictions, as they respect such lands, shall have been decided or adjusted subsequent to such grants, or any of them, shall, on application to the Senate, be finally determined, as near as may be, in the same manner as is before prescribed for deciding controversies between different States.

X.

Sect. 1. The Executive Power of the United States shall be vefted in a fingle person. His ftile shall be, " The Prefident of the United States of America;" and his title shall be, " His Excellency." [He shall be elected by joint ballot by the Legiflature.† He shall hold his office during the term of feven years; but shall not be elected a second time.

which election a majority
of the votes of the members prefent
to be required

to the Legiflature

Sect. 2. He shall, from time to time, give information to the Legiflature of the State of the Union: and he may recommend to their confideration such measures as he shall judge neceffary, and expedient: he may convene them on extraordinary occasions. In case of disagreement between the two Houses, with regard to the time of adjournment, he may adjourn them to such time as he shall think proper: he shall take care that the laws of the United States be duly and faithfully executed: he shall commiffion all the officers of the United States; and shall appoint ▬▬▬ in all cafes not otherwife provided for by this constitution. He shall receive Ambaffadors, ▬▬▬▬▬▬▬▬▬▬▬▬ He shall have power to grant reprieves and pardons; but his pardon shall not be pleadable in bar of an impeachment. He shall be Commander in Chief of the Army and Navy of the United States, and of the Militia of the feveral States. He shall, at ftated times, receive for his fervices, a compenfation, which shall neither be encreafed nor diminished during his continuance in office. Before he shall enter on the duties of his de-

FINISHING TOUCHES

The group was getting closer to a finished constitution, but there were still issues. The delegates discussed how the executive, or president, would be elected. There were many different ideas, including direct election by the people or election by political bodies such as the state legislatures or Congress. Finally, this debate ended in yet another compromise: the Electoral College.

Despite all the debate and compromise, some delegates weren't happy with the constitution at all. They didn't like how much power the federal government had, and they didn't like that the document didn't have a bill, or list, of rights for American citizens. In fact, delegate George Mason said he'd "sooner chop off his right hand than put it to the Constitution as it now stands."

A CLOSER LOOK

IN TIME, A COMMITTEE OF STYLE POLISHED THE WORDING OF THE CONSTITUTION. ITS MEMBERS INCLUDED ALEXANDER HAMILTON, JAMES MADISON, WILLIAM SAMUEL JOHNSON, AND GOUVERNEUR MORRIS.

THE ELECTORAL COLLEGE

The Electoral College, which is established by Article II Section 1 of the Constitution, is the process that elects the president of the United States. When people vote in a presidential election, they're actually voting for electors, or members of the Electoral College, who then vote for the president. Each state has the same number of electors as it has representatives in the House of Representatives and the Senate. Washington, DC, has three electors.

FIVE TIMES IN U.S. HISTORY, A PRESIDENTIAL CANDIDATE HAS LOST THE POPULAR VOTE BUT WON IN THE ELECTORAL COLLEGE. WINNING THE ELECTION, THIS MAP SHOWS THE RESULTS OF THE 2016 ELECTION OF DONALD TRUMP OVER HILLARY CLINTON.

ELECTORAL COLLEGE
- TRUMP (REPUBLICAN) 304 ELECTORAL VOTES
- CLINTON (DEMOCRATIC) 227 ELECTORAL VOTES

12
7
4
55
6
6
3
3
9
3
3
5
6
10
8
11
5
38
7
6
6
10
10
20
11
18
8
11
9
6
9
16
10
16
20
5
13
15
9
3
29
29
4
3
11
7
4
14
3
10
3
5
3
20
4

POPULAR VOTE
CLINTON 65,853,516
TRUMP 62,984,825

THIRTY-NINE
SIGNATURES

Finally, on September 17, 1787, the delegates met to sign the final version of the document they'd debated and labored over for months. However, not all 55 of the men who took part in the Constitutional Convention would put their **signatures** to it. In the end, only 39 delegates signed the new U.S. Constitution.

Some of the delegates had already left Philadelphia to travel back to their home states. Three men—George Mason and Edmund Randolph of Virginia and Elbridge Gerry of Massachusetts—refused to sign it because of what it didn't contain. They were unhappy that the finished Constitution, which gave so much more power to the federal government, didn't have a bill of rights. Some other delegates agreed with them, but signed the document anyway.

A CLOSER LOOK

ONE DELEGATE, JOHN DICKINSON OF DELAWARE, WAS
ILL ON THE DAY THE CONSTITUTION WAS SIGNED. HOWEVER, HIS
NAME IS STILL ON THE DOCUMENT. HE ASKED DELEGATE
GEORGE READ TO SIGN HIS NAME FOR HIM.

MASON AND THE BILL OF RIGHTS

George Mason wanted citizens' rights added to the beginning of the Constitution. When his fellow delegates defeated this proposal, he refused to sign the document. After the Constitution was ratified by enough states in 1788, Congress approved amendments to define certain rights of citizens and states. Ratified in 1791, the first 10 constitutional amendments are called the Bill of Rights. These amendments, drafted by James Madison, were heavily influenced by an earlier work of Mason's called the Virginia Declaration of Rights.

THE DELEGATES' NAMES WERE GROUPED BY STATE. THE OLDEST PERSON TO SIGN THE CONSTITUTION WAS 81-YEAR-OLD PENNSYLVANIA DELEGATE BENJAMIN FRANKLIN. THE YOUNGEST WAS JONATHAN DAYTON OF NEW JERSEY, WHO WAS 26.

RATIFICATION FIGHT

The U.S. Constitution was complete and signed. However, the fight was just beginning. According to Article VII of the Constitution, at least nine states had to ratify it, and that looked like it would be difficult. Feelings were strong on both sides. One side, called the Federalists, worked hard to win support for the new Constitution. They were opposed by the Anti-Federalists, who worked against it.

Both sides used writings and meetings to spread their opinions. Founding Fathers Patrick Henry, Samuel Adams, and James Monroe spoke against ratification. Perhaps the most well-known of the Anti-Federalist writers called himself Cato. He was probably New York governor George Clinton. On the side of the Federalists, the most famous writers were Alexander Hamilton, John Jay, and James Madison, who combined to defend the Constitution under the name Publius.

A CLOSER LOOK

THE ANTI-FEDERALISTS GREW INTO A
POLITICAL PARTY CALLED THE DEMOCRATIC-REPUBLICANS
AND LATER, THE DEMOCRATS.

THE FEDERALIST

Together, Hamilton, Jay, and Madison wrote 85 essays as Publius, starting in late 1787. Newspapers printed these essays, which were later collected and published in two volumes as *The Federalist*. In their writings, the three men explained the Constitution in detail, wrote about the weaknesses of the Articles of Confederation, and responded to critics. The essays were effective. In fact, Thomas Jefferson later called them "the best commentary on the principles of government ever written."

ALEXANDER HAMILTON WROTE MOST OF *THE FEDERALIST* ESSAYS. HE WORKED HARD IN HIS HOME STATE OF NEW YORK TO CONVINCE PEOPLE TO SUPPORT THE CONSTITUTION.

EDERALIST:

A COLLECTION

OF

ESSAYS,

WRITTEN IN FAVOUR OF THE

EW CONSTITUTION,

GREED UPON BY THE FEDERAL CONVENTION,
SEPTEMBER 17, 1787.

IN TWO VOLUMES.

VOL. I.

NEW-YORK:

PRINTED AND SOLD BY J. AND A. McLEAN,
No. 41, HANOVER-SCUARE.
M,DCC,LXXXVIII.

The first state to ratify the U.S. Constitution was Delaware, on December 7, 1787. Pennsylvania, New Jersey, Georgia, and Connecticut followed quickly. However, other states, including Massachusetts, hesitated. In the end, it was one more compromise that likely saved the Constitution. Federalists, particularly James Madison, agreed to add a bill of rights to the document.

Massachusetts, Maryland, and South Carolina then ratified the Constitution. On June 21, 1788, New Hampshire became the required ninth state to approve it, followed by Virginia and New York. North Carolina was twelfth. Rhode Island held out until May 1790—months after the new government had started. It'd been a long fight full of debate and compromise, but the United States had a new constitution, one approved by its original 13 states.

A CLOSER LOOK

AFTER NEW HAMPSHIRE RATIFIED THE CONSTITUTION, CONGRESS SET MARCH 4, 1789, AS THE DATE FOR THE NEW GOVERNMENT TO BEGIN.

THE BILL OF RIGHTS

In June 1789, James Madison introduced 19 amendments to Congress as part of a bill of rights. Congress sent 12 of these amendments to the states by September 1789, and by December 1791, the states had approved 10 of them. These amendments, the Bill of Rights, protect a number of individual rights belonging to the citizens of the United States, among them free exercise of religion and freedom of speech and of the press.

THIS DRAWING SHOWS A PARADE CELEBRATING NEW YORK'S RATIFICATION OF THE U.S. CONSTITUTION ON JULY 26, 1788. IT FEATURED A BOAT NAMED FOR FAMOUS FEDERALIST ALEXANDER HAMILTON.

TAKING EFFECT

Much hard work had been done, but now the new government had to come together as outlined in the Constitution. On January 7, 1789, the first presidential election took place. While the **inauguration** was supposed to be in early March 1789, cold, snowy weather kept it from happening until April, when enough members of Congress arrived to count the electoral ballots. George Washington was elected the first president with all 69 electoral votes cast, with John Adams as his vice president. With that election, the new U.S. government under the Constitution began.

Today, the U.S. Constitution is the oldest written national constitution still in use. It's been amended 17 times since the Bill of Rights, permitting changes such as outlawing slavery, providing voting rights to black Americans and women, and limiting presidential terms.

A CLOSER LOOK

ELECTORS IN 10 STATES CAST THEIR VOTES IN THE FIRST PRESIDENTIAL ELECTION UNDER THE CONSTITUTION. NORTH CAROLINA AND RHODE ISLAND HADN'T RATIFIED THE CONSTITUTION YET, AND NEW YORK DIDN'T CHOOSE ELECTORS ON TIME.

George Washington took office on April 30, 1789—in New York City, which was then the nation's capital. Philadelphia, Pennsylvania, was the capital from 1790 until 1800, when the capital finally became Washington, DC, which it remains today. President Washington himself had chosen the area in 1790, but the government didn't move there until 1800. The city is named for George Washington, and it's within an area called the District of Columbia (named for Christopher Columbus).

THIS IMAGE SHOW GEORGE WASHINGTON'S INAUGURATION AS THE FIRST PRESIDENT OF THE UNITED STATES IN APRIL 1789 AT FEDERAL HALL IN NEW YORK CITY.

THROUGH THE YEARS

Now that the U.S. Constitution has been in effect for more than 230 years, it might be odd to remember that it wasn't always a respected document. Nearly every clause was fought over and debated. Delegates—many of whom disagreed with each other strongly—had to compromise again and again to come up with a document that would be acceptable (though not ideal) to all.

Today, you can still visit the document and the other Charters of Freedom at the National Archives Museum. The U.S. Constitution wasn't, and isn't, perfect, but it was the first of its kind in many ways. This document was designed to put checks on the powerful while promising rights for all citizens, making the United States a "more perfect" union.

27 AMENDMENTS

As of 2020, there are 27 amendments to the Constitution. The last of these was approved in 1992. The Twenty-seventh Amendment requires that any change to Congress salaries can only take effect after the next election in the House of Representatives. This was actually the second of the amendments sent to the states by Congress all the way back in 1789. It wasn't approved by enough states for more than 200 years.

TIMELINE OF THE U.S. CONSTITUTION

MAY 14, 1787: THE CONSTITUTIONAL CONVENTION OPENS IN PHILADELPHIA, PENNSYLVANIA.

MAY 25, 1787: THE REQUIRED NUMBER OF DELEGATES ARRIVES AT THE CONSTITUTIONAL CONVENTION TO OPEN PROCEEDINGS.

MAY 29, 1787: EDMUND RANDOLPH PRESENTS THE VIRGINIA PLAN.

JULY 16, 1787: THE DELEGATES APPROVE THE GREAT COMPROMISE.

JULY 24, 1787: THE COMMITTEE OF DETAIL IS NAMED.

AUGUST 6, 1787: DELEGATES BEGIN TO DISCUSS THE DRAFT OF THE CONSTITUTION.

SEPTEMBER 17, 1787: THIRTY-NINE DELEGATES OF THE CONSTITUTIONAL CONVENTION SIGN THE CONSTITUTION.

DECEMBER 7, 1787: DELAWARE BECOMES THE FIRST STATE TO RATIFY THE CONSTITUTION.

JUNE 21, 1788: NEW HAMPSHIRE BECOMES THE REQUIRED NINTH STATE TO RATIFY THE CONSTITUTION.

MARCH 4, 1789: U.S. GOVERNMENT UNDER THE CONSTITUTION GOES INTO EFFECT.

JUNE 8, 1789: JAMES MADISON INTRODUCES 19 PROPOSED AMENDMENTS—A BILL OF RIGHTS—TO CONGRESS.

MAY 29, 1790: RHODE ISLAND IS THE LAST STATE TO RATIFY THE CONSTITUTION.

DECEMBER 15, 1791: THE BILL OF RIGHTS IS RATIFIED.

THE U.S. CONSTITUTION, THE SUPREME LAW OF THE NATION, WAS WRITTEN AND RATIFIED IN LESS THAN A YEAR.

A CLOSER LOOK

ANY NEW AMENDMENTS TO THE U.S. CONSTITUTION MUST BE PASSED BY A TWO-THIRDS MAJORITY VOTE IN BOTH HOUSES OF CONGRESS OR BY A CONVENTION BY TWO-THIRDS OF THE STATE LEGISLATURES. THEN, THE AMENDMENTS MUST BE RATIFIED BY THREE-FOURTHS OF THE STATES.

GLOSSARY

attorney general: the chief law officer of a nation or state who represents the government and serves as its top legal adviser

clause: a part of a legal document

commerce: the large-scale buying and selling of goods and services

Continental Congress: a meeting of colonial representatives before, during, and after the American Revolution

convention: a gathering of people who have a common interest or purpose

debate: an argument or public discussion. Also, to formally discuss or argue an issue.

document: a formal piece of writing

draft: a document before completion. Also, to write a first version of a piece of writing.

inauguration: a ceremony marking the start of someone's term in public office

parchment: an old kind of paper made from the skins of sheep or goats

popular vote: the votes of all people in a country or state, rather than the votes of a group such as the Electoral College

signature: a person's name in that person's handwriting

zeal: a strong feeling of eagerness or interest

FOR MORE INFORMATION

BOOKS

Buckley, Jim, Jr. *Alexander Hamilton*. New York, NY: DK Publishing, 2019.

Demuth, Patricia Brennan. *What Is the Constitution?* New York, NY: Penguin Workshop, 2018.

Lassieur, Allison. *Building a New Nation: An Interactive American Revolution Adventure*. North Mankato, MN: Capstone Press, 2019.

WEBSITES

The Great Compromise of 1787
www.thoughtco.com/great-compromise-of-1787-3322289
Learn more about a compromise (one of many) that saved the U.S. Constitutional Convention.

Meet the Framers of the Constitution
www.archives.gov/founding-docs/founding-fathers
Find out more about the 55 delegates of the Constitutional Convention and the 39 who signed it.

INDEX